Nature ABC

MALLARD
PRESS

MALLARD PRESS

First published in the United States of America in 1989 by Mallard Press
An Imprint of BDD Promotional Book Company, Inc.
666 Fifth Avenue
New York, NY 10103

"Mallard Press and its accompanying design and logo are trademarks of
BDD Promotional Book Company, Inc."

Cover photo: Bill Ivy
Typesetting: Artwords
Printed and bound in Italy

Nature ABC

A is for Alligator.

**Alligators spend their days floating
in the water and lying in the mud.
At night they hunt for food, and they
sleep all winter long.**

Bb

B is for Bear.

Bears swim and climb trees. They eat almost everything and like to be alone.

Cc

C is for Chipmunk.

Chipmunks use their cheeks for lunchboxes and live in holes in the ground. They are really nuts about nuts.

Dd

D is for Duck.

**You can tell ducks by their quacks.
Ducks float on the water, paddling with
their wide, webbed feet.**

Ee

E is for Elephant.

Elephants use their long noses for drinking and taking a shower. These are from Africa. You can tell by their ears. Indian elephants have small ones.

Ff

F is for Frog.

Frogs catch bugs with their long, sticky tongues. Their babies are tadpoles, which look like tiny fish.

Gg

G is for Giraffe.

Giraffes eat leaves from the tops of trees. Their newborn babies are six feet tall.

Hh

**H is for Horse,
of course.**

**Horses used to be wild and roamed all
over the world. Today they are used
for riding and racing and farming, and
live in barns.**

Ii

I is for Iguana.

The iguana has a long green tail
and spines down its back. Iguanas live
in trees and eat plants deep in the
forests of Mexico.

J is for blue Jay.

Its wings and tail are bright, bright blue. It has a wild cry like a hawk's.

K is for Kangaroo.

Kangaroos keep their babies in their pouch and hop all over Australia. Males are called boomers, females are flyers, and babies are always named joey.

Ll

**L is for Lion,
king of the beasts.**

**Lions live in Africa in groups called
prides. You can tell that this one is a
male because it has a mane.**

Mm

M is for Monkey.

Monkeys are always on the move, climbing through the trees. They have fingers like yours, and some monkeys can hold things with their tails.

Nn

N is for Nuthatch.

**Nuthatches climb down tree trunks
headfirst. They wedge nuts into cracks
in trees and peck the nuts open.**

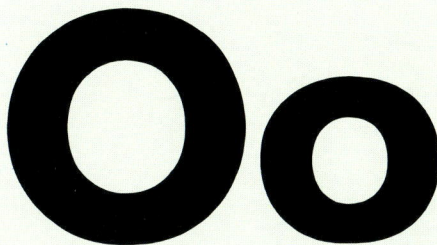

**O is for Owl,
who hoots in the dark.**

**By day owls sleep in their hiding
places. At night they chase mice, frogs,
bugs, and birds for their supper,
gliding silently through the air.**

Pp

P is for Panda,
who lives in China.

Pandas climb trees and eat bamboo.
There are not many pandas left in
the world.

Qq

Q is for Quail.

Quails travel in flocks called coveys. They lay eggs in large batches called clutches in nests on the ground.

Rr

R is for Raccoon.

Raccoons come out at night to look for food. Often they find it in your garden or your garbage can.

Ss

S is for Seal.

Seals live in the sea and have flippers
for feet and ears inside their heads.
You can tell this one is a baby
because of its white coat.

T is for Tiger.

A tiger is like a lion with stripes but no mane. Tigers cannot see or smell very well, so they hunt for food with their ears, creeping silently.

Uu

U is for Urchin,
which lives in the sea.

Its mouth is on the bottom, and wiggly
spines are on the top. Urchins walk
on tiny tube feet.

Vv

V is for Vulture.

Some vultures are six feet wide when they spread their wings. With their keen eyesight, they can see everything below them from high in the sky.

W is for Walrus,
which is bigger than a seal.

Walruses have tusks and cheekpads
with long whiskers. They live in the sea
and have almost no hair at all.

**X is for foX,
a cousin of the dog.**

**Fox families live underground until the
children grow up. Then they sleep in
the grass, with their tails curled around
them for warmth.**

Yy

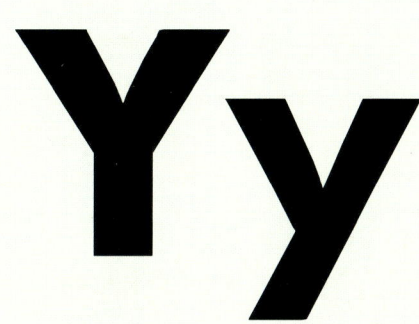

Y is for Yak.

**Yaks live high in the mountains.
They provide milk and butter, and
carry heavy loads on their backs.**

Zz

**Z is for Zebra,
a horse with stripes.**

**Zebras live on the plains of Africa in
huge herds, and can run like lightning.
Their enemy is the lion.**

Photo Credits

Bruemmer, Fred: seal
Cribb, James M. (First Light): urchin
Dennis, Lisl (The Image Bank Canada): yak
De Visser, John: horse
Dorval, Didier (First Light): monkey
Dwyer, Janet F. (First Light): iguana
Ivy, Bill: frog, kangaroo, lion, nuthatch, owl, raccoon, tiger, cow
Lang, Aubrey: elephant
Lankinen, Wayne: quail
Lynch, Wayne: bear, chipmunk, duck, giraffe, panda, vulture, zebra
McLeod, Peter (First Light): jay
Metro Toronto Zoo: alligator
Milne, Brian (First Light): fox, walrus